# David  Thru Schizophrenia: Healing Awareness

David LaChapelle

# The Thorn in the Flesh

And lest I should be exalted above measure by the abundance of the revelations, a thorn in the flesh was given to me, a messenger of Satan to buffet me, lest I be exalted above measure. Concerning this thing I pleaded with the Lord three times that it might depart from me. And He said to me, "My grace is sufficient for you, for My strength is made perfect in weakness." Therefore most gladly I will rather boast in my infirmities, that the power of Christ may rest upon me. Therefore I take pleasure in infirmities, in reproaches, in needs, in persecutions, in distresses, for Christ's sake. For when I am weak, then I am strong.

## 2 Corinthians 12:7-10 New King James Version (NKJV)

# CONTENTS

Introduction                                   7


Chapter 1: Instability                         9

Chapter 2: Group Therapy                      33

Chapter 3: Individual Therapy                 47

Chapter 4: Finding Acceptance                 59

Chapter 5: Moving Forward                     77

Chapter 6: Night Out                          99

Chapter 7: Birthday Party                    113


Conclusion                                   125

# Introduction

For most of my life, I had been laying a foundation for the future by getting an education, so I would have a successful and comfortable life. Then, Schizophrenia hit me in my late 20's like a freight train and all that I needed was good health to accomplish my ambitious goals had been taken away from me. While recovering from Schizophrenia again I had to live for a future day when I could live a so called normal life. I took 17 years to come to this point of acceptance I have Schizophrenia and unless someone comes up with a cure or God performs a miracle I will probably have Schizophrenia my whole life. That does not mean that my condition will not improve, it just means I am ready for the journey and not seeking a final-result of being free from Schizophrenia to feel complete or loved.

David's Victory Thru Schizophrenia: Healing Awareness is a book about perseverance while overcoming the odds of unfair circumstances and poor mental health to restoration and wholeness. I have journaled the damaging emotions I experienced and my perspective towards myself, others, and life over four difficult years. I uncover the hidden truths about myself when I was mildly psychotic with Schizophrenia, as my medication switches towards newer anti-psychotic medications did not work out. Included is the revealing of personal blind spots about myself and detailed intimate conversations from my psychiatrist appointments spread throughout the book that occurred during one and a half years, group and individual therapy sessions. As I heal I find acceptance and my life moves forward as I socialize, enjoying the companionship of a new friend and becoming active in the community.

I was motivated to write about overcoming my challenges in my life and health, because I feel that sharing my insight could help others out and bring awareness about what it is like to live with Schizophrenia being a born again Christian. I hope you enjoy my open and honest account of this part of my life and may my experiences reveal to you what you need to pay attention to in your own life or in the life of someone else.

# Chapter 1: Instability

I moved from my hometown of Toronto in 1996 to attend Carleton University in Ottawa. I was enrolled in the Electrical Engineering Program because I had spent three years studying and training to be an Electronic Technologist at Seneca College. I found Physics, Calculus, Chemistry and Algebra too difficult for me and after failing these Engineering pre-requisites I transferred into the Political Science program a year later. I thought I could do a better job running the country than the present politicians at the time, so I volunteered at Parliament Hill the legislative branch of the federal government for a month, for the Member of Parliament governing where I was living.

In my third year, when school was out for the summer holidays, I got a job at the Brick. The Brick is a superstore that sells the latest furniture and electronics and my position with the company was an office worker. I would enter customer's invoices into the computer so they could receive their purchases either from the back warehouse or to be delivered at a future date. The job consisted of one month's training and I only lasted one month after training. I was let go by the manager because I was exhibiting strange behavior: I would take my lunch break when I thought I should have it and was performing poorly on the job as my mind became more clouded and unfocused as each day went by. I was also expelled from University for having poor academic standing for three years. There was nothing holding me to live in Ottawa anymore as my friends were moving back to their hometowns and I was having trouble adapting to the Conservative mindset of Ottawa.

My world was falling apart in the summer of 1999 so I moved back home to Toronto and, unknown to me I was coming down with some mental illness. I was undiagnosed and my family recognized my strange behavior because I was avoiding them. They were determined to get me psychiatric help but I never got along with my family and I thought they were the ones that were crazy. I did not know which way to turn because I did not want live with my family so I lived out of my car for a month. I then went to church with the intentions I would declare in public I am the savior of the world, instead I became a born again Christian.

I was 27 years old when I signed my life over to Christ and the next day my family got a court order to have me committed to the mental health ward at North York General Hospital. I stopped at my mother's apartment to get some food and I was intercepted by my dad and brother accompanied by two officers from Toronto Police. I was taken to the hospital in the back of a police cruiser against my will and I stayed there a week. I had met a girl named Angela, a mental health patient at the hospital and hired her lawyer. Angela's lawyer got me out on a legal technicality, that the hospital did not put my rights in writing there was proof I agreed to further treatment after the required seventy-two hours.

For six months we travelled across Canada by car and when I came back home my family discovered where I was living and had me committed to a psychiatric hospital in downtown Toronto called the Clarke Institute. I got out of the hospital on the second day because Angela pretended to be my wife and I gave the speech of my life to the staff convincing them I am being persecuted. Two months later I committed a crime and was locked down in a psychiatric facility in Toronto and had treatment forced upon me which included 6mg of the antipsychotic medication Risperdal. After my three months at the Center for Addiction and Mental Health I received my official diagnosis of Paranoid Schizophrenia and then moved to a depressed small town having no friends and being a dependent. I was overtaken by my new reality being alone with my dad, learning about being a new Christian and dealing with Schizophrenia. My world became very closed in as I was a stranger in town, my mental health was poor and people were leery of me.

In my first year in Lindsay I just spent my time lying on the couch. I would go to the convenience store to buy cigarettes every other day and that was it. After my first year living in town I went for walks by myself but felt that everybody was looking at me because I was paranoid and the town I was living in everybody knew everybody's business. After living in the apartment for two years my brother bought me a Yellow Labrador puppy for some company and moved into a house with a nice backyard and outdoor deck. I sold Calvin a year later because I found he was too energetic and difficult for me to look after. I had two friends in town during my four years residing in the house but not anyone who was close. In my sixth year living in Lindsay, I volunteered at a computer shop and Staples for four months but I found that working was too stressful on me. I had trouble getting up in the morning to go to work and my health was not to where I was comfortable interacting with the public. I wrote about this part of my life in my exhilarating first book: David's Adventure with Schizophrenia: My Road to Recovery.

In 2006, my mental health improved enough I moved to a nearby better town Peterborough. In 2007, I attended Trent University and in 2010, I moved out on my own into an apartment and in 2011, I graduated with a Bachelor of Arts in Psychology. I was stable while living in my new town enough I handled going to University part time and earning good grades. It was not until I switched my anti-psychotic medication Risperdal to Abilify in 2012, that my emotional rollercoaster began. I transitioned into a maximum dose of 30mg of Abilify, which I took in the morning and did not have to be taken with a meal. My Risperdal of 6mg was decreased 0.5mg every month, till I took no Risperdal, and just Abilify. While I was experimenting with this new medication, a few people in my neighborhood were mean by putting me down right in front of me, and were probably gossiping about me behind my back. I felt hurt and wounded because there was no way I could get back at them for what they did, so the only thing I knew to do was to protect myself by isolating myself in my apartment. My dad noticed my strange behavior and forced me to go to the mental health ward at Peterborough Regional Health Centre. Abilify was not strong enough on its own in combating my fears and paranoia even though it gave me more physical energy and boosted my mood.

At the hospital in 2013, I switched to 180 mg of Zeldox and 2 mg of Risperdal. Three weeks later I was released from the mental health ward and six months later I became employed full time as a customer service technical representative. At this time, I was not communicating with my family and rid myself of a friend I had. I distanced myself from my family because I was mildly psychotic and could not handle their emotional dysfunction and the friend I had was not accepting of me and I did not fit in the crowd he hung out with. The stress of working under pressure for two months in the summer and being alone made Zeldox to become ineffective. In the fall time, I visited and communicated with my family again. My dad and his girlfriend Betty live in town and my mother and brother and Nancy my dad's previous girlfriend and Daniel live out of town. My mother and brother and my distant friends would visit irregularly so I was alone a lot. Zeldox made me very drowsy, as I had to take Zeldox twice a day. I took 60mg of Zeldox with breakfast and 120mg with dinner and my Risperdal before bedtime. Zeldox made my heart race and pound irregularly, otherwise I have no heart problems.

In 2014, I volunteered to check myself into the hospital and had my Zeldox switched to Latuda and published my second book David's Journey with Schizophrenia: Insight into Recovery. From 2014 to 2016, I have been on 60 mg of Latuda and had my Risperdal increased from 1mg to 4mg in 1mg intervals because I found Latuda was not doing anything and I had to depend more heavily on Risperdal as time went by. I found right from the beginning that Latuda made me feel depressed on top of making me feel mildly drowsy after taking it with dinner.

Of instability in my medications I was alone a lot, because I was emotionally hurt, fearful, paranoid and resentful towards others. I magnified out of proportion the offenses of others by rehashing in my mind what others said or did while stewing in a critical spirit. I would put a lot of unnecessary pressure on myself by holding a grudge against others. It seemed there was no way I could right the wrongs done and this set me back emotionally. I thought by being bitter and having an unforgiving attitude I was getting revenge on others not knowing I was only hurting myself. I allowed the negativity of a few to consume me and I thought I had to deal with my issues on my own.

My love tanks were running on empty. I had nothing of myself to give and because of my deprived state, others could sense that, and kept their distance from me emotionally. I lacked the proper emotional support from those close to be able learn to trust people again and connect with others. I was frustrated, because I knew what was happening, but I could do nothing about it. I thought my dad and his girlfriend were holding out on me because it seemed they were giving me mixed signals by being indifferent and nice at other times and I felt lost in the world. I thought that others could choose to accept or reject me because I wanted the approval of others, but resented them, because I gave them that power over me.

I was full of fear, paranoia and anxiety, so I tried to predict the outcome of a situation or behavior of a person so I would attain the desired result I expected to be left alone and be safe. I was fighting against being judgmental towards people by looking down on them, as I unconsciously thought if I would reject them first they could not reject me, but it would always come back. I could not let my guard down and this led people to be tentative around me because they did not want to hurt or offend me. I was offended and hurt by this dynamic because deep down inside I wanted so much more: I wanted acceptance. I thought I was above my fears, anxiety and paranoia trying to deny and ignore Schizophrenia's existence in my life but I was not.

I expected God to pick up the slack, but he never did, because I had the problem. I had a lot of pride because I wanted to be independent from God and was fighting against him every step of the way. I harbored un-forgiveness and bitterness towards almost everybody, including God, because of my unmet needs. I could not distinguish who was for me or who was against me and I thought others made me feel invalidated. I had built up a protective wall around me to shelter me from the potential that others have to emotionally hurt me. I tried to overcompensate for my insecurities by thinking I was above and better than others. I did not realize that others were respecting the wall I built around myself and probably well knew I was dealing with some emotional wound. I did not know that others could not see through my protective shell that deep down inside I wanted to be outgoing. I thought I was loving and friendly but I was sending the message to others through my attitude to not mess with me. I wanted others to connect with me past my closed off and self-righteous attitude because I thought everybody owed me.

I thought I deserved much better out of life and would worry how am I ever going to get out this rut I am in. I wondered how am I ever going to survive when my dad passes away, especially since I feel so limited and disabled. I felt vulnerable and inadequate in myself and thought there was no way I could ever trust God to provide for me. I did not recognize immediately that my medications were not working and thought I was feeling fearful and paranoid was just part of having Schizophrenia. I thought God was not on my side because he did not let me have my way. I wanted to be part of the normal world and have a normal life and I figured that if God is not giving me that right now that he is holding out on me. I thought God forgot about me and that if I continued placing my hope in him he would probably let me down. Life would pass me by and there would be no way to get it back when I got older. Those were my fears at the time because I was so self-centered thinking about myself all day long. Being alone so much provided me the opportunity to be preoccupied with myself and what others were not doing for me.

I felt powerless, because I knew no other way to get people to be open. I was frustrated, because I could do nothing to change that fact not realizing I was pushing people away from me. I blamed God for not healing me from Schizophrenia and improving my life. I then tried to manipulate God to see my viewpoint that I am a victim, that others hurt me, and wanted to continue hurting me and were in the wrong. I cursed God for not delivering from my pain and suffering and for not protecting me when I thought he should of. I wanted God to change others to suit me or to give me financial blessings so I could meet new people who would be understanding, loving and supportive. God did not make either desire a reality in my life, so I thought he either has no power or does not care about me. I did not trust God because of the trials and tribulations I had endured, and the suffering I was experiencing, but what was I supposed to do at this point in my life.

I have been seeing my psychiatrist every three months since I arrived in Peterborough in 2006. Sometimes when I am not feeling that great my doctor will see me more regularly, but for the meantime this has been my schedule with Dr.T. In

2016, ten years later I felt comfortable enough with my doctor to reach out for some help. On the date of May 3rd/2016, was my first doctor's appointment where I shared my struggles with life that I realized I cannot handle life on my own and need some support.

Dr. T: Why are you so guarded?

Me: I am alone too much and (Action) shedding a tear.

Dr. T: Are you paranoid you do not go out?

Me: I have nowhere to go.

Dr. T: Why don't you volunteer.

Me: I am working on that.

Dr. T: Did you quit smoking?

Me: I am still smoking.

Me: I smoke because I have anxiety caused by being bored and have nothing to do during the day.

Dr. T. (Showing) Confusion!

Dr. T: Did Champix work for you?

Me: It is hard to occupy the day without smoking because I have nothing going on.

Dr. T: Are you depressed?

Me: No.

Dr. T. (Showing) Excitement!

Me: (Thinking) Dr. T. is just dying to prescribe me some anti-depressants that I do not want or need.

Me: I talk to my mom and brother twice a day. I text my friend Daniel now and then, talk to my friend Nancy over the phone once a week but do not talk to my dad anymore.

Dr. T: I am concerned that your dad might call and bother me you are sick like the last time you stopped talking to your dad.

Me: It is different this time because I am talking to my mother and brother which I was not before. My dad and his girlfriend do not say Hi or talk when I think they should which I find rude and ignorant. They make me feel crazy because of how they treat me and I don't deserve that.

Dr. T. (Showing) Not concerned.

Me: (Thinking) Dr. T. probable thought I have enough social friends and family contact to be ok.

Dr. T. You should keep your distance from your dad and his girlfriend. You have a complex family and I will see you in one month's time.

Me: Goodbye.

Dr. T: Goodbye.

During the month of May and the beginning of June I was still feeling alone and rejected by my neighborhood and not being treated right by my dad and his girlfriend. I harbored un-forgiveness and bitterness but did not want to feel those emotions. I did not know how to change them to make others treat me better. A month later, on the date of June 7th/2016, was my next appointment with Dr. T.

Me: Hello Doctor.

Dr. T: Hello.

Dr. T. (Showing) Anger and abruptly spoke.

Dr. T. Sit down.

Me: (Thinking) This will be a long 15 mins.

Dr. T: You were not feeling that great during our last visit did you get your volunteer position.

Me: I got a volunteer position and I did it on my own. My employment counselor did nothing for me and ended my dealings with him.

Dr. T: What is your family situation?

Me: I do not visit my dad, but I talk to him by phone every three days for about a few minutes, and my brother was up for two weeks from Toronto.

Dr. T: You have to keep your guard up with your brother.

Me: He tried to treat me like a kid and I put him in his place. When I visit with my brother you usually have to put him in his place initially, then you are ok throughout the rest of the visit, otherwise you have to put up with him all day long. For example: In my brother's care on our way to downtown to the volunteer office he told me to not let the police check paper get out of my hand and not blow out the window, and I told him I am not an invalid. My brother said he never said that I was invalid and I told him to not treat me like a kid.

Dr T: Some families they treat each other like kids.

Me: (Thinking) Whatever.

Dr. T: Do you still smoke?

Me: Yes.

Dr. T: How much do you smoke?

Me: About ¾ of a pack a day.

Dr. T: Do you smoke indoors?

Me: Yes.

Dr. T: It's difficult to quit when you smoke indoors. You never said why Champix did not work for you?

Me: (Thinking) I already told her during our last visit why.

Me: It is hard to pass the day when you have so much time on your hands and when I quit smoking time is frozen. It feels as if I am stuck in time.

Dr. T: That is addiction.

Me: (Thinking) She has no clue what is like to deal with Schizophrenia because I remember when I smoked when I did not have this disease it was not that difficult to quit.

Me: My neighbors are low life's and they ask me personal questions that are none of their business and talk behind my back. My family mistreats me and that I have lost my trust in people.

Dr. T. It seems you don't trust people.

Me: I do not. What is a person supposed to think in people when surrounded by idiots? I put up a wall around me to protect myself from others because I thought they were hurting machines.

Dr. T: (Showing) Forcefully recommended.

Dr. T: Attend the peer support group at the hospital

Me: Yes, I will.

Dr. T: Attend the peer support group.

Me: Yes:

Dr. T: Attend the peer support group.

Me: Yes.

Me: (Thinking) Is she hearing me.

Dr. T: I will see you in six weeks.

Me: Goodbye.

Dr. T: Goodbye.

During the next six weeks, nothing much changed except I had a revelation I was judging others and that all my relationship problems were because of what was going on inside of me. I was excited to tell Dr. T. what I had discovered that remained so hidden from me all these years. I still did not attend group therapy yet and attended my appointment with Dr. T on July 19th/2016.

Me: How are you?

Me: (Observation) Dr. T. looked me up and down with a quick analytical glance.

Dr. T: How are you?

Me: I feel good.

Dr. T: The last time you were mistrustful of people.

Me: That is over as I took the speck out of my eye

Dr. T: That is biblical.

Me: Yes, it is.

Me: I do not see and focus on the faults and flaws of others anymore. I try to see the good in people like I used to before I moved into this neighborhood. Now I am more careful with who I hang around and keep company with.

Dr. T: Focusing on others faults gives them power over you.

Me: I know

Dr. T: It can wear you down.

Me: (Showing) Laughing

Me: I know.

Dr. T: What are you doing?

Me: I volunteer at MusicFest.

Me: People yell at you, but they don't mess with me because I am big guy.

Dr. T: Do you get paid?

Me: No.

Dr. T: That is how they can keep the concerts free.

Dr. T: How are your medications working?

Me: I feel good, but I am tired after my dinner dose of 60mg of Latuda. I go to bed early when I take my 4mg of Risperdal at bedtime.

Me: (Thinking) I will not tell her I take 1mg of Risperdal at noon and 3mg at bedtime.

Dr. T: When do you go to bed.

Me: Around 7pm.

Dr. T: That is early.

Me: I get up around 5am.

Me: When I was on 6mg of Risperdal I had no motivation and it was difficult to shower because I had to rush just to go in slow motion.

Dr. T: Other drugs do not work as well as Risperdal but they have less Parkinson symptoms than Risperdal.

Me: I visit my dad and his girlfriend, but they do not bother me anymore and I am more relaxed around them because I am not judging them anymore, even though they may treat me ignorantly.

Dr. T: Your blood work is due in October and I will see you in three months.

After my appointment, I went to visit with the secretary to book my next visit which I do every time.

Martine: Hello David.

Me: Hello.

Me: Someone must of stole the books again in the waiting room.

Martine: I have couple of extras of books in the office I will put in the waiting room.

Me: There will be people from my neighborhood with mental health issues and probably come here for their appointments and would want them, especially since I sold my first copy of my second book in the neighborhood to a couple in my building. It would interest the people of the neighborhood, because I talk about me and some of my dealings with some and now the word is probably spreading.

Martine: I liked your first book because it is a real story and that you must feel like a celebrity. You probably look back and cannot believe that you did those crazy things.

Me: For sure.

Martine: Bring two books next time you will come here.

Martine: People borrow the books but they never bring it back. Maybe I should get their names and phone numbers to get them to return the books.

Me: You should have your own library card for the clinic.

Martine: (Action) Laughing.

Me: I have read so many books, earned a psychology degree and experienced so much with Schizophrenia I need to have some outlet to express myself and cannot hold it all inside.

Martine: Your first book would make a great movie and I hope it happens.

Me: A film director who has bipolar liked a book about bipolar and he made the authors book into a movie.

Me: I wait for an email everyday hoping someone wants to make my book into a movie. The movie about bipolar stars Katie Holmes.

Martine: Who would I want to play you in the movie?

Me: My dad thinks Ed Norton would be good because he plays real crazy roles and I thought Winona Ryder would be good for Angela my girlfriend at the time because she looks like her.

Me: See you later.

Martine: Bye David.

# Chapter 2: Group Therapy

On the date of September 7/2017, I reached out for help and get the emotional support I needed by attending group therapy at Peterborough Regional Health Center. I have been holding inside so many ill feelings I thought this would be the best way to get them off my chest so I can move on with my life and heal. There were seven people in the group including me and the counsellor. There was coffee, juice, bran muffins and a vegetable tray with dip.

Counsellor: We have new people to the group and I would like everybody to introduce themselves.

Barbara: Hi I'm Barbara.

Frank: Hi I'm Frank.

Me: Hi I'm David.

Ann: Hi I'm Ann.

Jessica: Hi I'm Jessica.

Bob: Hi I'm Bob.

Counsellor: Ok who would like to start first.

Barbara: I will go first.

Barbara: My husband goes back to work soon and I must cook dinner. He has been on employment insurance for some time and it is running out. My life will change when my husband goes back to work because I cook for our children.

Frank: I got Schizophrenia when I was 17.

Me: I got Schizophrenia at 27 and that I did a lot of things from 17 to 27.

Frank: I live with my mother and look after her in her elderly years. I have a car which is good and can get around but parking fees at the hospital is expensive.

Counsellor: Why don't you park on the side street I advised you too.

Frank: I did last time and got a parking ticket.

Me: Over the past few years I have been very unstable because I switched to Abilify from Risperdal for over a year and Abilify did not work for me. Then I switched to Zeldox and after a year Zeldox did not work for me either. I am just now getting stable by being on Latuda and Risperdal.

Me: I have lowered myself by coming to this group because I have little of an emotional support network from family and friends. There is just no one I can confide in about what I am going through because they do not understand what it is like to have Schizophrenia and do not want to understand.

Me: I have realized I have to focus on goals I can achieve and are based in reality not grandiose ideas about my life because I had so much hope and ambition for my life. Now I just want a friend or a girlfriend on disability benefits and going through the same things I am going through.

Frank: What you are saying David is an exact mirror of my life and what I am going through. I have no energy to worry about life anymore.

Me: I gave up worry too because it was driving me crazy and not getting me anywhere.

Me: Everything I had been through I understand why God did what he did but wonder when is God going to reward me for putting up with all the crap over the years.

Me: I was on a dating website looking for a girlfriend. I was thinking what am I going to do with a so called normal girlfriend with a job and probably wants to have children. That I would have to tell her I have Schizophrenia and I am on disability benefits from the government.

Me: I was living in Ottawa going to Carleton University and had three groups of friends: my study circle was Political Science Majors my house party circle were friends from Northern Ontario and my clubbing circle were International students. I volunteered at Parliament Hill the federal legislative branch of the Canadian government and had 100 of acquaintances because I lived in residence for my first year and socially networked.

Me: Then I came down with Schizophrenia and I had to live with my dad in a small town with no friends and nobody would bother with me because I was new to town and everybody knew I had no friends so that made it even worse.

Barbara: Why did you move from Ottawa?

Me: I got kicked out of Carleton University because of my poor grades.

Jessica: You have to reach out to people.

Me: What Reach out to the cashiers at Walmart?

Jessica: No, people in the group.

Me: I played volleyball a few years ago but I met nobody back then.

Jessica: Do you think that Peterborough is friendly?

Me: No.

Me: I went to my local church and nobody even acknowledged my existence.

Barbara: I have had the same experience.

Frank: I agree.

Me: I am from a middle-class family where people had careers and jobs while living in the suburbs. Now I can't talk to my neighbors because they are always backstabbing and gossiping about each other and I am not used to that.

Jessica: I am from Etobicoke a suburb of Toronto and that I understand what you are going through because my friends have jobs.

Me: I have no emotional support and do not want to spend all my time alone but have to have some time alone to write. Which I am writing my next book.

Me: I look at Peterborough as a small town and not a city.

Me: I thought I could meet people by working but I cannot handle a job and no one will give me one anyways because I have no recent work experience on my resume.

Me: If I worked at Walmart I would last only a week.

Counsellor: See everybody next week.

Group was finished and I then went to the secretary's office.

Martine: When will you want to see the Doctor.

Me: I was at group.

Martine: Oh, yes.

Me: I would like to sign up for another group maybe the life transition group that takes place not far from where I live.

Martine: Ok I will inform Sophia you want to attend the transition group.

Me: Thanks, see you later.

Martine: Bye David.

On the date of Sept 13/2016, I attended my second group therapy session. There were eight people including me and the counsellor and again there was coffee, juice, bran muffins and a vegetable tray with dip. There were a few familiar faces but there were two new people I had never seen before. I decided this time I would play it cool and wait until most clients have spoken before I took my turn.

Counsellor: We have new people to the group and I would like everybody to introduce themselves.

Barbara: Hi I'm Barbara.

Maria: Hi I'm Maria.

Susan: Hi I'm Susan.

Ann: Hi I'm Ann.

Jessica: Hi I'm Jessica.

Joe: Hi I'm Joe.

Me: Hi I'm David.

Counsellor: Ok who would like to start first.

Maria: I got my original birth certificate and will meet my family for the first time this weekend. I was adopted because my mother was an unwed mother. I am nervous and hope that things go well so wish me luck.

Everybody: Good luck Maria.

Joe: My Netflix and Sony PlayStation are not working so life is boring and I find it difficult to pass the day. Instead I listen to music all day and sleep. I take Seroquel five times a day.

Me: Do you find that taking your medications so regularly that it makes you drowsy.

Joe: (Showing) Acted like he did not know what I was talking about.

Jessica: I went to the senior's club and ate dinner there. I had dessert which I rarely eat because it was part of the meal. I was overwhelmed by being around so many people and was very tired from playing card games. My neck and wrists hurt because the game we were playing I had to keep my neck and hands up. When I came home I was constantly remembering the names of the people I met at the club.

Me: I feel better since last time I got things off my chest. I have been watching Charles Stanley's six-part series on the internet about healing damaged emotions.

Me: (Thinking) I felt that no one was listening or cared.

Me: I used to want to fix people to be the way I want them to be and others would stay the same. It was not until I gave up trying to change people and my expectations that others became what I wanted them to become. That is such a retarded relationship.

Counsellor: (Showing) displeasure by frowning and gestured that the word retarded is a word I should not be using in group.

Me: (Feeling) I felt a smothering sense of guilt from others in the group.

Me: (Action) I tried to shake off the awful guilt feeling and cried.

Me: Others in my neighborhood are backstabbers and gossipers and I have seen how low people can go.

Joe: (Action) Gets up from his chair.

Jessica: Where are going Joe?

Joe: I'm leaving.

Me: I do not know where to go to meet good people.

Jessica: David you can go to the book store, the farmers market or mall.

Me: (Thinking) I will still go there by myself.

Me: I know what places to avoid now to stay away from the low life.

Jessica: The best thing for you David is to get out of the house to fix your situation. Then she said I could go to the Royal Canadian Legion.

Me: (Thinking) She is probably right but the legion is full of people who are much older than me.

Me: I just want to meet normal people.

Counsellor: (Showing) Displeasure by frowning that normal was a word I should not be using in group.

Counsellor: I will see you guys next week.

Counsellor: (Action) Cleaning the coffee maker.

Counsellor: David I would like to talk to you are you in a rush to go somewhere?

Me: No.

Counsellor: (Action) Sat in front of me.

Counsellor: David you are way to negative.

Me: The town is not open to new people and only like their own kind.

Me: I cannot get a job here.

Counsellor: Most people working at the hospital are from out of town.

Counsellor: How long have you lived here in Peterborough?

Me: 10 years.

Counsellor: (Showing) Shock.

Counsellor: I have only been here 3 years.

Counsellor: David you should not come to group anymore. You are having a negative impact on the group by running down the town and that individual therapy would be better for you.

Counsellor: Did Dr. T. advise you to come to group?

Me: Yes.

Counsellor: I will talk to Dr. T. to get you some individual therapy.

Counsellor: You have to change David.

Me: So, that low life's, won't bother me anymore.

Counsellor: You have to change for you. I do not have the power to change you.

Me: People in this town are living back about 50 years. They marry their high school sweetheart and have three kids and buy a truck and do not need to meet anyone new.

Me: If I had enough money I would move to Toronto.

Counsellor: I have somewhere to be right now and can talk no longer.

# Chapter 3: Individual Therapy

On the date of September 15th/2016, I got a phone call from Mike the social worker at the hospital.

Mike: Hello can I speak with David.

Me: This is David.

Mike: I was referred to speak with you through the group counsellor.

Mike: It seems some issues need to be dealt with and would you like to meet with me.

Me: That is true Mike.

Me: I went to group therapy with the expectations I could let my feelings out but that was not the case.

Mike: Your Right David that seems like the logical thing to do.

Me: I was friendly to the town but got no reciprocation and my neighbors were friendly but in time some turned on me and started backstabbing me. That hurt me because I was trying to be good to them but I guess many were jealous of me.

Me: As I was going through the challenges with my neighbors I changed my medication to Abilify for a year and a half and that did not work out and then I switched to Zeldox and that did not work out as well so I just isolated myself in my apartment and kept to myself.

Mike: Was there a time when people were friendly to you.

Me: Not really.

Me: I find this town to be conservative.

Mike: There are conservative sentiments in this town.

Me: Since few people reciprocated to my friendly gestures I just closed up and not talk to people.

Mike: There seems some stigma you dealing with.

Me: (Thinking) How did he know.

Me: Yes.

Me: I wrote two books and that everyone knows that I have Schizophrenia in my neighborhood.

Me: My family never talked about Schizophrenia or how to deal with it while I was recovering.

Mike: Schizophrenia is taboo in your family.

Me: A lot of stigma.

Me: For many years I had no friends and God was my only support and friend.

Me: (Action) Crying.

Mike: I am sorry to hear that David.

Mike: I do not want to upset you because I have to end our conversation and let's save the good stuff for when we meet. How is September 20th/2016 on a Tuesday.

Mike: Morning or afternoon.

Me: Afternoon.

Mike: 1:00pm or 3:00pm.

Me: 3 O'clock is good for me.

Mike: My office is across from where group meets.

Me: (Thinking) Tuesdays at 1:00pm is when the group meets so I chose the 3:00pm time slot because I did not want to run into anybody from the group because I felt embarrassed at how I was so negative during the two sessions of therapy.

Mike: Look forward to seeing you.

Me: Me too.

The next day after talking to Mike I had a rollercoaster of a day between feeling good and feeling guilt, condemnation and shame. It was so overwhelming that I broke down and cried for fifteen minutes in my living room. I then told God off that I hate him and that I cannot deal with having Schizophrenia anymore, and that I do not want to have it anymore, and for him to take it away from me. After being broken I felt an immediate sense of freedom from my dysfunctional emotions and felt peace I have never experienced before. I decided at that moment I would have nothing to do with God anymore and distanced myself emotionally from believing and depending on him. I felt a separation from God, but there was a lot of freedom in that decision, because the world had given up tormenting me, because I felt a freedom from the world and the complex nervous energies I usually feel were gone.

The next day after breaking down in my apartment I felt a sense of wholeness I have never experienced before. The next day I felt great and I went to Walmart to get a few things. I felt calm and relaxed that I influenced others to be the same and put people at ease. For three days now I feel normal and have no anxiety. On the date of September 20, 2016, I had my individual counselling appointment with Mike the social worker. I met Mike in the psychosis clinic waiting room and we shook hands and introduced ourselves to each other and then Mike led me to his office.

Mike: Have a Seat.

Mike: I heard you wrote a book.

Me: Yes.

Mike: Someone read it and said it was good.

Me: Which one did they read because I wrote two books.

Mike: The one in the waiting room.

Me: I have faced stigma from family and neighborhood and my medication switches with Abilify and Zeldox did not work out. I isolated myself for a few years because people were being so cruel.

Mike: What is the evidence you are facing stigma?

Me: One neighbor used to be friendly towards me and now he is tentative.

Me: My dad tells me he does not talk because he does not want to bother me and I am become bitter simultaneously because he is not talking. My dad told me that because my family does not talk at family gatherings I cannot base my life on them.

Mike: David have you ever thought of saying: Why are you tentative Stanley.

Me: I cannot be bothered.

Mike: It seems you have had a tough time at group.

Me: I was under that assumption you go to group to share your feelings and let it all out.

Mike: You were intense and influenced the group greatly probably in a negative way because you were running down the town.

Mike: What is Schizophrenia?

Me: I think it is the ego rushing to the surface of the personality.

Mike: That makes sense because the ego is all about fear and paranoia often exhibited in people suffering from Schizophrenia.

Me: When you are born again you are given a fresh slate in life and become a new creature. I remember how I used to be before being born again and I was a lot like my dad.

Mike: What is the ego? Is it like what Freud said about the ego, id and superego.

Me: I do not know but the ego is pain and suffering and everything that God is not and is evil and makes you feel threatened for no reason.

Me: It is easy to see the ego in others because many people are so unaware of themselves they express it in anger by reacting aggressively with an imagined threat by arguing or exhibiting violence.

Mike: That is true. I was backing out my car from my driveway I almost backed into two teenagers. I saw them at the last moment and stopped. One guy freaked out and all I could do was say sorry but I was too mindful of myself to react in anger.

Me: That event in your life is a gift from God as an opportunity to make your ego smaller by starving it.

Me: The more people hurt you or you feel hurt and the more you do not feed your ego the smaller it gets, but if you have one moment where you break down and react, it will take many successful events to overcome to get back to where you were before the breakdown. Reacting to your ego creates a negative energy field and momentum that needs to be winded down.

Me: People are like sandpaper polishing you into a beautiful ornament.

Me: It is easy to see ego in others, but too see it in yourself is harder, because it is so deceitful, sophisticated, and unnoticeable because the patterns they show seem to be a part of how you are and who you are.

Mike: When I go to the grocery store I am sensitive to people's face expressions and some people are friendly and some people are not.

Mike: Being sensitive we think we can read minds.

Me: That is my problem I think I know what people are thinking.

Mike: Maybe people are thinking different than what you think they are thinking.

Mike: I am a people watcher. Are you a people watcher?

Me: Yes.

Mike: Does it feel you can read people's minds?

Me: I am very sensitive to facial expressions and body language.

Mike: (Action) Pulling out a piece of paper from his desk cupboard and handing it to me.

Mike: Is this what you are talking about?

> Me: (Reading) An old Cherokee is teaching his grandson about life. "A fight is going on inside me," he said to the boy.

"It is a terrible fight and it is between two wolves. One is evil – he is anger, envy, sorrow, regret, greed, arrogance, self-pity, guilt, resentment, inferiority, lies, false pride, superiority, and ego."
He continued, "The other is good – he is joy, peace, love, hope, serenity, humility, kindness, benevolence, empathy, generosity, truth, compassion, and faith. The same fight is going on inside you – and inside every other person, too."

The grandson thought about it for a minute and then asked his grandfather, "Which wolf will win?"

The old Cherokee simply replied, "The one you feed."

Me: Exactly.

Me: I have no emotional support because of the stigma I am facing and that is why I write books. My first book is emotionally heavy, and the second one is less weighty, but now that I have recognized my problem I am facing stigma, my third book will be even more lighter and full of awareness.

Mike: Do you want to go to group again?

Me: Sure, I can smooth things over with group.

Mike: Do you want an appointment with a therapist?

Me: I thought you are one.

Mike: No I am a social worker.

Me: Maybe later.

Me: I broke down emotionally after talking to you over the phone.

Mike: Was it because of talking to me.

Me: No.

Me: I broke down crying for fifteen minutes and told God where to go and that I do not want to have Schizophrenia anymore and gave it to God.

Me: Immediately my anxiety was gone that I was dealing with for sixteen years and thought nothing of it until the next day while I was lying in my bed I felt a healing presence of peace and felt wholesome.

Me: I went to Walmart and when I was there I calmed down everybody there because I was so content and relaxed and influenced many people in a positive way as I could see it by the look on their faces they were amazed by me.

Me: Women are more sensitive to the fact that I had no ego and I said guys are still more ego driven then women.

Mike: If you saw someone across the street you knew and they avoided you and walked away what would you think.

Me: It depends if I trust the person or not, but usually I would think maybe they forgot to put money in the parking meter or maybe they do not like me. I do not think about stuff like that anymore.

Mike: We had a good talk and I will remember this conversation for a while.

Me: Take care.

Mike: You too.

# Chapter 4: Finding Acceptance

I believed my life did not work out the way I wanted it to because of having Schizophrenia. If I just had good health, I could work full time and could meet people. I was stuck in that thought pattern for the past four years because I reasoned with myself that I either had to have it all or nothing. I was hard on myself, because I thought it would get me somewhere If I was, and it made me anxious and discontent. I was unaware that I was putting too much pressure on myself to do more in life and to not be alone. I hated being vulnerable and dependent upon God and other people and thought if I could be independent and strong I would have financial security and be free from worry.

I felt I did not measure up to my standards in life and that one day if I kept reaching out to God he would bless me enough he would make up for lost time. I had been trying to improve myself and was trying to reach God by doing and being good so God would accept me and make me normal. I thought I had to be normal to accept myself and I rejected myself because I could not accept that I am living with Schizophrenia. I rejected others because they are not perfect, because I thought I would be perfect if I did not have Schizophrenia. I hoped that by attaining normalcy, I would be complete and then I could move on in my life.

I thought God was doing nothing, because my life and health was not improving. I felt helpless to do anything on my own and developed a victim identity because I could not accept myself. I thought the only way I could get ahead was for God to do something miraculous in my life. I lacked direction and was getting frustrated because I did not know which turn to take. I was not grounded in my present circumstances and what I could do to make my life better from where I was. I wanted to skip years and steps ahead in life to be in some dream life away from everything I knew. When God did not perform the miracle I was hoping for I gave others the responsibility to meet my needs. I never knew what the outcome would be because people are so unreliable and would experience anxiety and feel overwhelmed.

I thought others were against me, trying to stop me from reaching my destiny, and felt stuck in life, because I could see no improvements in my health and the way others related. In the world of psychology, there is a term called emotional incongruence, it means being in a state of dissatisfaction and uncertainty because your real self does not match up with your ideal self. For many years, I lived being unable to accept myself because I could not accept that I have Schizophrenia. I wanted to overcompensate for my perceived flaws by having some fantasy life that would erase all the negative effects of having Schizophrenia.

I expected God to bridge the gap between my real and ideal self by performing a miracle in my life. I wanted to be above others and the ones who had hurt me emotionally so I could have redemption in my life. It was insanity living this way because I was sacrificing the present for some fantasy future moment. I had a lot of pride and could not settle myself down to think of having an average and humble life. I became harsh on myself because I knew there was so much more I could do in life if only given the chance. The only way I thought I could ever reach my potential, was if God healed me from Schizophrenia. I rejected others, because they seemed they had no part to play in me reaching my new life I desired.

I had to give up the fight against God to get him to do what I wanted him to do. When I gave Schizophrenia over to God in that trying day in September 2016, I forgave, and chose to surrender more of myself to God. Immediately my dysfunctional emotions such as fear, worry, doubt, bitterness and resentment melted away and a transformation took place. The world then opened up to me as my attitude changed and I had a deeper connection with God when I saw God as being good. It made me more relaxed around people because It stopped me from thinking that the world owes me and I accepted myself. That is when the walls I had built around myself came crashing down.

On the date of October, 18/2016, I attended my psychiatrist appointment with Dr. T. where I was excited to tell the Doctor about my newfound discovery.

Dr. T: How are you?

Me: I feel great.

Dr. T: (Showing) Dr. T seemed bewildered at how I could be feeling great.

Me: I have no fears anymore and people are real friendly.

Dr. T: Does that scare you that people are friendly to you?

Me: No, just that it is foreign.

Dr. T: Your protective shell is down.

Me: (Thinking) I guess I have no protective shell anymore.

Dr. T: People often feel threatened by people with a protective shell around them because others cannot read them.

Dr. T: You have come a long way. You wrote two books.

Dr. T: How did your protective shell disappear.

Me: I gave it to God and he took my fears.

Dr. T: That happened fast. Sometimes that happens when spiritual forces are involved.

Dr. T: Are you scared that people are friendly to you?

Me: No, just that it is foreign.

Dr. T: Do you have fears of having no shell?

Me: The fears are gone that is why I have no shell.

Dr. T: Be careful. You will put up a shell again, it will come back.

Me: I remember when I first came down with Schizophrenia I had a thick protective shell.

Dr. T: Because you are trying to make sense out of everything.

Dr. T: Are you on the same level of medications.

Me: Yes, I am taking 60mg of Latuda and 4mg of Risperdal. I take 1mg in the afternoon and 3mg at bedtime.

Dr. T: I think it is time for your bloodwork.

Me: Can I go to either the clinic or hospital laboratory?

Dr. T: Yes, get your bloodwork done within a week.

Me: Ok.

Dr. T: I will see you in three months in January sometime.

Me: Ok.

Me: Goodbye.

Dr. T: Goodbye.

I am getting stronger and stronger as each day goes by. Fears about being abandoned, alone and rejected don't cross my mind anymore. I know others are not perfect and if someone intends to offend I know God has a purpose in it and that I am not a victim. What I have discovered now that I am free from fear and have had my protective shell and self-righteous attitude dissolved, that people I interact with are comfortable, open and friendly towards and around me. I do not worry about life anymore, because I know I am where I supposed to be going through what I am experiencing.

I am more relaxed and comfortable with myself and do not pressure myself and others to live up to some unrealistic expectations I used to have. I thought that by being gentle on myself that life would pass me by, but I discovered that the opposite is true. Life is easier to deal with when you are easy on yourself, because it takes a lot of stress and energy fighting against things in life beyond your control. Accepting myself makes it easier to accept other people the way they are and in return accept me for who I am. I need not be perfect, and other people need not be perfect to receive love and to be accepted by me. That is the only way I can have meaningful relationships in my life as I learned to accept myself and then others.

On the date of January, 17/2017, I rescheduled my psychiatrist appointment with Dr. T. because there was freezing rain in Peterborough and it was too icy to travel. I rescheduled my appointment with Dr. T. to Feb 21$^{st}$/2017. My Doctor cancelled my Feb 21/2017, appointment and it was changed to March 21$^{st}$/2017, and then my Doctor cancelled my March 21$^{st}$/2017, appointment and rescheduled it for April 25/2017. Here is my Doctors appointment with Dr. T. on April 25/2017.

Dr. T: Sit down.

Dr. T: How are you?

Me: Good.

Dr. T: Well, it has been a long time since you have seen me. I think it was in October. Fill me in.

Me: Well, I am on 7mg of Risperdal and have rid myself of Latuda.

Dr. T: Why did you get off Latuda? It was not doing anything?

Me: Yes, it made me feel blue.

Dr. T: Depressed?

Me: Yes, depressed.

Dr. T: What level of depression mild, medium or severe like you want to hurt yourself?

Me: Mild depression.

Dr. T: You have been on Latuda for two years.

Me: I know but it is difficult to know if a drug is working or not.

Me: I thought that maybe the sedative effects of Latuda made me feel that way.

Dr. T: Feeling sedated differs from from feeling depressed.

Me: Abilify was the opposite it boosted my mood.

Dr. T: Abilify did not work for you.

Me: Yes, not on its own.

Dr. T: Yes, Abilify should be taken with Risperdal.

Dr. T: Did you get your doctor to write a prescription or did you do it yourself?

Me: No, I just filled the prescription of 4mg of Risperdal you gave me before and the new one of 4mg simultaneously.

Dr. T: I do not see how Walmart Pharmacy can do that because they are supposed to cancel the old prescription in place of the new one.

Me: They can be funny.

Dr. T: Not funny when doing that.

Dr. T: Do you smoke?

Me: Yes, about ¾ pack a day

Dr. T: Does the 7mg affect your motor skills and do you walk slowly?

Me: No.

Dr. T: When you started the 7mg of Risperdal did you feel the depression leaving.

Me: No, when I got off Latuda I stopped feeling depressed.

Dr. T: How did you get off Latuda?

Me: Cold turkey. I just stopped taking it.

Dr. T: Do you talk to your father and brother?

Me: Yes.

Dr. T: They seem to bother you when you are not feeling too well.

Me: Yes, I know.

Me: I do not know what the connection is between not feeling too well and being bothered by my family.

Dr. T: Do you socialize?

Me: Yes, I talk to my neighbors, which I have not done for a long time.

Dr. T: Do you have trouble going out?

Me: No, sometimes I have nowhere to go.

Dr. T: Is it your mom or Nancy that supports you emotionally?

Me: Yes, Nancy is always supportive and consistent.

Me: My dad, brother and mother used to offend me but not lately.

Me: I will volunteer at a retirement home once my police check gets finalized.

Dr. T: Good.

Dr. T: Are you still writing a book?

Me: Yes, I am on Chapter 4 and have about 50 pages so far completed.

Me: Here is the disability tax credit form for you.

Dr. T: I will fill it out the best I can but the government always sends me forms asking questions back to be answered.

Me: No problem.

Dr. T: It seems your self-managing your medications that is not too traumatic and that is good.

Me: I knew Risperdal worked for me in the past so it was not a gamble.

Me: Risperdal is different this time.

Dr. T: How?

Me: There is not a war going in my head between Schizophrenia and the medication.

Dr. T: That is strange.

Me: I am getting better.

Me: Before if I took Risperdal before bedtime it would knock me out to sleep but it is more gentle now.

Me: Taking Abilify, Zeldox and Latuda must have changed my brain to make Risperdal work better.

Dr. T: Medications do not permanently change the brains neurotransmitters.

Dr. T: Have you heard voices or had hallucinations.

Me: No.

Dr. T: I will see you in three months.

Me: Ok.

Me: I like your hair. (Dr. T. got a new short hairstyle.)

Me: Enjoy the weather.

Dr. T: Laughing.

I realize now, that God is more concerned with changing me from the inside out, then he is with improving my circumstances. That is why he has allowed the many trials and tribulations in my life. No matter how often I petitioned God to change others to suit me, he kept up the pressure to change me. My un-forgiveness put a lot of pressure on myself for many years, because I wanted others to accept me and for God to use and bless me. It was not until I had a change in attitude and saw God as behind and in control of everything in my life I view God as good. That is when the mistreatment from others did not bother me anymore and I saw them as a tool to shape me to be more like Jesus. That is when I removed myself from being self-centered and became Jesus centered where I am not the focus of everything going on. I am not easily offended anymore and do not think that others can read my mind to supply my needs because only God can know what I need in life.

For the past four years I have spent a lot time by myself and felt rejected, because I felt that no one wanted to bother with me. I thought that other people had the power to accept me, not realizing how I feel with other people depends on how I feel about myself. The world did not look right because I was spending so much time by myself and because I felt rejected, I became hard on myself and rigid in my thinking, as my thought process consisted of all or nothing. I would say to myself I have to do this or I have to not do that, there was no in between. I was always focused on the character flaws of others and what others were not doing for me. I was giving too much attention to the ego of others and felt responsible to protect myself from them. I thought I was more important than I was because of my relationship with God and was self-righteous using my faith as an excuse to have an exaggerated opinion of myself. Now that I trust God, I do not question everything and everybody trying to constantly figure everything out. I do not focus on how others should treat me but on how I treat others.

There was no way God would intervene in my life if I am in his way. If am worrying and trying to change people and fix my problems on my own there is no way that God can get in and solve the situation without hurting me. I surrender all care and control over to the Lord and look forward to what he will do in my life. I know God will make me a testimony to bring others to him especially those close. I know God has a plan for my life no matter how insignificant I may feel and what my life circumstances may be, and I see the love of God everywhere, and opportunities to help others out are everywhere. I have settled down and trust God more than before. Not that I am trying harder to trust him, it just is easier to trust, because a change has taken place inside of me. I have good and bad days, but for the most part I do not take the inconsistencies of human behavior personal anymore.

Now that I am stable on 7mg of Risperdal and am not fighting to be someone other than what I am,

Schizophrenia has no hold on me as much as it used to. Schizophrenia does not define who I am anymore, and all I can do is just be myself and enjoy my peace having Jesus at the center and following his will for my life. I am not focused on my limitations and compare myself with so called normal people and what other people have that I do not have. I do not have condemnation, guilt or shame and I do not feel hurt by the world. Some days I feel I do not even have schizophrenia and the testing period God was putting me through seems over with. My identity crisis seems over with and others are treating me the way I want to be treated. That I have faith in Jesus and not faith in myself has made a big difference in my life. Before I was trying to get God to do what I wanted him to do and for him to give me favoritism instead of trusting God to provide for my needs and giving me favor. I was working myself to death with self-effort trying to get God on my side instead of getting on God's side. I was trying to qualify for God's blessings, now I realize I deserve nothing and am grateful because I am just alive. I was always frustrated because I was trying to get God to do something for me he has already done.

# Chapter 5: Moving Forward

On the date of May 9/2017, I tried to quit smoking through nicotine replacement therapy. I was taking 21mg of the patch, which I would put on in the morning, and 2mg of cinnamon gum, which I would chew whenever I had a craving. I know it is hard on the heart to both be on the patch and chewing the gum, but I took my chances even though it could have been detrimental to my health. What inspired me to quit this time was, I noticed when I got up out of bed during the night to use the washroom, I was out of breath for ten minutes after I came back to my bed. I reasoned with myself that I have to make a change, because I cannot live like this anymore.

My quitting smoking program only lasted five days, because I was coming down with a wicked cold and the stress from quitting smoking and having a cold was too much for me to deal with. I was worried that the extreme stress would make my Schizophrenia act up and I would have a psychotic episode. I had a stuffed up nose and was coughing up green-mucus and my airways were constricted even more than before. I had no choice but to cut down my smoking by 75 percent, because I could not breathe anymore.

Of suffering, I did not even think about having Schizophrenia, because I was so preoccupied with my nasty chest cold. The accuser "Satan" that was always judging me and my interactions with myself and others was quiet. I felt no condemnation, guilt or shame while having this cold, and no fears or paranoias or feeling wronged by others. The monkey on my back, telling me wherever I went that I had Schizophrenia and nothing is any good, was gone. Something different happened when I came down with this cold: I realized how human and vulnerable I am, and that I depend totally upon God to heal me, to get out of almost dying with pneumonia. I had to muster up enough energy to go my doctor and get some anti-biotics. At the clinic I was coughing profusely and I looked like I had been through hell, so my doctor prescribed me anti-biotics and an asthma inhaler. Each day being on Amoxicillin I felt better, but I took the ten days to finish my pills to heal. I was coughing a lot and it hurt me when I did.

There was when I was sitting in the gazebo outside my building with my neighbors Dillon and Mikey and was sitting down having a cigarette when I experienced a coughing spell. I coughed so hard that I could not breathe and passed out in the chair I was sitting on. All I remember is seeing a bright light but I did not walk into it, then I felt someone touching my shoulder and gently calling my name. I felt I was at the bottom of the ocean when I was unconscious when I felt Mikey's touch and heard his voice way up there on the surface. I tried to come up in my mind to where Mikey was, and when I woke up, Mikey told me I blacked out for a minute and I could not believe what I was hearing. When I woke up, I took 20 minutes to come to reality, and thanked Mikey for saving my life.

I went out into the gazebo two days later and I ran into Dillon again. He invited me up to his apartment for a cup of coffee. In his apartment Dillon was telling me that that Thomas, a resident from Dillon's building is not a good person to associate with. After having my cup of coffee, I gave Dillon my telephone number and we hung out every day. We would go out for a bite to eat or just hang out in his apartment. A few weeks later I drove Dillon to pick up some groceries and to get his guitar amplifier fixed at the music store and pick up some music records. Dillon is a great musician and is good with the guitar and singing. He likes singing John Prine and knows many songs. He listens to Country classics or Classic rock, whereas I listen mostly to Christian music.

Dillon has Schizophrenia like myself, and I understand where he is coming from, because I have been there myself. Dillon takes a needle for his Schizophrenia medication once a month and is taking pills for depression and bipolar. Dillon had been through more psychotic episodes than I have and has been in the mental health ward many more times than myself, but his last episode was 6 months ago, because they discontinued the medication he was on for a long time and had to start a new medication. Dillon's medication switch led him to be placed in the mental health ward again and his doctor told him it might take a year to adjust to his new medication. On his new medication, Dillon sees reality more than before and he finds it a difficult to digest this new normal.

Dillon is going through the same things I go through, such as stigma and struggled with being alone a lot. When I started hanging out with Dillon he had a lot on his mind and had things he wanted to get off his chest he needed to release by being listened to without judgement. I have been through adversity in my life, so I am good at comforting Dillon and he is company for me and somebody to relate to and do things with. After being friends with Dillon I feel normal as I feel my love tanks are full and I do not feel alone anymore. I used to worry about being alone and how I would occupy the day and how and when I would meet a friend to talk with and do things with.

I quit smoking again on June 15/2017. The first few days and first week went good because I kept myself busy running errands with Dillon I had no time to myself to think about smoking and experience nicotine withdrawal. I was on the patch and gum just like last time and had an interrupted sleep for the first week because of nicotine withdrawal and had vivid and weird dreams because I kept the patch on for twenty-four hours. I chewed 8 pieces of nicotine gum each day for the first seven days while on the patch and then I stopped chewing the gum and had only the patch for 7 more days. I bought more gum after I finished the 14 days of the 21mg patch and chewed the 2mg cinnamon gum sparingly or whenever I had a nicotine craving. I was coughing up mucus and my breathing became a lot better every day. On the 12$^{th}$ day of quitting smoking I ran for a minute from my car in the parking lot to my apartment building and I did not get out of breath. What got me through the tough times quitting smoking and to stay smoke free was I had many people supporting me to quit. Nancy kept telling me I can do it and Dillon and his mother Josie kept advising me to keep up the good work and do not give up because the benefits of being smoke free is worth it. My family supported me quitting smoking but they were more tentative because I failed quitting smoking so often before.

On June 15/2017, the same time I quit smoking I received a telephone call from the volunteer coordinator from the retirement home I applied for. Susan apologized for taking so much time in getting back. She told me she was busy processing the volunteer student program. I replied, I figured you were busy with the volunteer student program because I had seen the advertisement in the local paper. We set up my orientation for June 27/2017, Tuesday at 11:00 am.

My orientation went smoothly, as Susan went over Ontario law regarding long term care facilities and the rules of the residence. She went over the codes such Code red: What to do in a fire and code yellow: What to do when there is a missing person in the building. She asked me if I have experience pushing people in wheelchairs, and I told her no. She said she will show me how to push a wheelchair my next shift, and then she showed me the volunteer lounge room, where I would log my hours worked, and in the cooler weather hang up my jacket. Susan showed me around the building and then she asked what day and time and for how long I would volunteer for. I told her Tuesdays and Thursdays in the afternoon for two hours is suitable for me, and she looked at the activity schedule for the residents and said that most positions are filled by students, but when September comes along there would be more for me to do when the students go back to school. She said that I could volunteer in the games and activity room helping residents get to and from games and helping them with playing the games and would I like to start July 6/2017, next Thursday from 3:00 to 4:30 pm. Then she escorted me out of the building and I walked home before it rained. I found that my lungs were in better shape when walking to the retirement home and up the stairs at the facility, but I found I still have more healing to do, because I was a little out of breath, when I really should not be. I talked to my dad after work and he told me he is proud of me for volunteering, and he told me I would enjoy it, and my mom told me I would like it because I can socialize and talk to people.

July 4/2017, in the evening the devil opened up on me and I felt a heavy pressure and a lot of anxiety over me. This feeling was telling me that the only way to relieve myself from the pain was to have a cigarette. I prayed to God, but it seemed he was not there, and all I said to the devil after weighing the pros and cons of smoking in my head, was you will just have to kill me, because I am not going back to smoking. I thought the pros to smoking would be: I would not have to suffer any more pressure and anxiety and the cons would be: that I would have to spend money on cigarettes, I would let down my family, friends and neighbors, the pain and suffering I endured quitting up to his point would have been for nothing and I could not breathe again if I smoked again. I decided that the way I am feeling will pass and there is no way I am going back to smoking no matter what. The next morning: I woke up early around 3:30 am refreshed and had a solid sleep and felt great after a night of hell.

I was getting ready grooming myself and eating breakfast when on July 6/2017, I got a call from Susan the volunteer coordinator from the retirement home that the lady I was supposed to work with today will not be in and that I will start next week same day and time. I was glad that my shift had been cancelled, because that gave me time to pick up my car in garage having the driver's side window fixed. I took the car in to have the power corrected in the instrument panel, but it was too expensive to fix, so I told the mechanic to forget about it. When I went to pick up my car, it was supposed to be ready, but it was not, so my dad and myself went out for coffee around the corner from the garage, until the work was completed 30 minutes later. After that, I just relaxed at home and waited for the evening to set in. After I took my bed time pills around 9:00pm I felt an evil presence and was experiencing again a lot of anxiety. If I had cigarettes in my apartment I would have gone back to smoking because the pressure was so strong. It was obviously a satanic attack but I could do nothing but to pray and wait for the storm to pass. I felt uncomfortable for three or four hours and then I settled down when the evil presence went away. I went to sleep minutes after that, but the next day I felt worn out because it was such an energy and emotional draining experience I went through the night before.

July 9/2017, I had strong nicotine craving and was tempted to go out and buy a pack of cigarettes because my mind was so foggy and unable to focus while experiencing anxiety. I said to myself you cannot go back to smoking, and every time I had quit before I gave up and would go back to smoking, so I told myself it will pass and that the cravings are not permanent. So I went to Walmart and bought 105 pieces of cinnamon 2mg nicotine gum. When I got home I chewed 3 pieces and felt a lot better. Then, I called Nancy and told her about my close call with going back to smoking, and she supported me, saying do not give up and you can do it.

July 11/2017, I felt anxiety, having an unfocused mind, experiencing evil nervous energies from my neighbors in the hallway outside my apartment door. When I was smoking before, I never felt these ill effects, and that is why I realized that I have to go back to smoking, because it just makes me feel normal and is my emotional support that eliminates my anxiety and nervous energies. I said to myself: if I can just limit myself to a few cigarettes a day I will be fine. Many people do not realize that smoking for those with Schizophrenia makes them feel normal and that is why so many of us smoke. I know I am letting a lot people down by going back to smoking, but I just have to do what makes me sane, content and happy.

July 13/2017, I started my volunteer position at the retirement home, and I met Susan at her office at 3pm. She directed me to Jennifer running the activity games for the residents. Two residents introduced themselves, but otherwise the residents in the room were quiet and a few residents noticed this and said why is everybody so quiet. The room was hot and humid and it made me sweat profusely. My polo shirt was soaked with wetness and sweat was even dripping on the floor from my forehead. I was wearing jeans and after setting up the plastic bowling pins for one hour Jennifer told me I could wear shorts for next time. It was hard on my back bending over to pick up the pins and the plastic bowling ball, but after 30 minutes my back strengthened and did not hurt anymore. Some residents were in wheelchairs and everybody enjoyed themselves and bowled a good game. A lady in a wheelchair came to the activity room half way through the residents bowling session and she immediately starred at me singing Hallelujah out load and her daughter visiting with her was surprised and I was amused. This resident had to use the ramp to launch and direct the bowling ball, because she did not have good use of her arms, and could not throw it, and did well in her bowling score.

When bowling was over Jennifer told me to take Gary to other side of the building on the same floor in his wheelchair. Then I told Jennifer: I will be going to the outside patio on the fourth floor to cool off and five minutes later Jennifer retrieved me. She then took me to introduce me to Eileen and told her I would help her with her tablet, skype, facetime and email simultaneously around 4:30pm next Thursday. Eileen shook my hand gently and Jennifer and I went back to the office. The secretary there asked if I knew Angela and Donny and I said I do, because she knew them, and because she knew I knew Betty their mother who is my dad's girlfriend. Jennifer said Donny was wild and I told her: I heard that. Jennifer told me I could go now, because I told her before, that I was only there until 4:30 pm. I went to 5th floor and signed the volunteer time sheet and picked up my jacket and came home. I felt good about myself after work like I accomplished something productive and had a purpose in life and felt needed and wanted.

July 20/2017, was my next shift at the retirement home and it went well. I waited in the office for Jennifer and while waiting I talked to the student volunteer coordinator about how Microsoft Word does not have good headings and how I would like my titles to stay in place and not move up and down when I either write something new or taking words out. I was introduced to Carol by the secretary as she was to be who I would be working with that day. She told me we could play bowling with the residents and I told her I already did that last week and it is hard on my back. The residents did not seem to have as much of a good time as the last time, except for Rosemary having a good time said in front of Carol in Italian "Bella" meaning beautiful to describe me. I played it cool and pretended I did not know what that word meant. After the bean bag toss I met up with Eileen and showed her how to use the computer. She was a quick learner, but she was having trouble using the mouse, because she could not see the cursor moving around the screen. We looked up cookie recipes and what was new in the news, and I looked up the Toronto Blue Jays score for yesterday's game at the request of Eileen who told me to look up something I wanted to. Then Eileen wanted to know how to email, and I told her she had to sign up for an email account. She inquired does that cost anything, and I told her you can pay for email but there are lots of free email out there so she could email her family. I was there two and a half hours in total, and came home after helping Eileen with the computer.

The next day I sold my e-bike for $600 and went out bought a new electric shaver and couple of dress casual pants one black and the other grey. Then I went to Dillon's place and we were talking about our illnesses and how we are doing so good and he said that I am doubly blessed to have equal education and life experiences, where most people either have one or the other. I thanked him for the compliment and said to him there is a war going on within us between the world and God and that we have to choose which side we are on and pointed out that it is better to be with God because we can give all our problems to him. The next day July 25/2017, I went to pick up my pants being hemmed up and then went to my psychiatrist appointment with Dr. T.

Dr. T: Please sit down.

Dr. T: I will be right back I just have to get your chart.

Dr. T: How are you feeling? (Observation) She looked right at me for a long moment when asking that question.

Me: Good.

Dr. T: It has been since April since last time. Did you change your medications? Because every time we meet you have changed your medications.

Me: No, I am still on 7mg of Risperdal and it is working good.

Dr. T: Have you seen your family doctor?

Me: I have to because it seems I am growing muscle and I should not and do not know why.

Me: I just bought clothes today because I do not fit into my pants anymore.

Me: I was 40 inches in my waist 6 years ago and 4 years ago my waist was 42 inches and 2 years ago my waist was 44 inches and now my waist is 48 inches.

Me: I do not eat a lot and I do not exercise that much and I should not be so large. Maybe my thyroid is acting up or something.

Dr. T: Your test results came back good and we did that in October and do not test again for some time.

Dr. T: You have to be careful about diabetes because Risperdal makes you vulnerable to it.

Me: My grandmother on my dad's side had it and diabetes runs in my family.

Dr. T: You do not have to be overweight to get diabetes you can get it even if you are skinny.

Dr. T: You should see Dr. U. your family doctor and he might connect you with a dietician or discover what is wrong.

Me: I was 2 times extra-large a few years ago and now I am 5 times extra-large in shirt size.

Dr. T: Do you talk to your family?

Me: I do not visit with my Dad in town that often but I talk to him twice a day.

Me: I talk to my mom and brother once a day and Nancy every four days and Nancy is going to Greece for a holiday for the month of August.

Dr. T: You do not talk to Nancy as much as you used too.

Dr. T: Your family do not seem to bother you when feeling well?

Me: I know.

Me: I have a friend Dillon. We do things together like get a bite to eat out or go shopping. We support each other because we both have Schizophrenia. I hang out with Dillon when I am not volunteering at the retirement home.

Dr. T: How do you like volunteering at the retirement home?

Me: People are friendly and nice. I help out in the games and activity part of the residents being active. The residents were excited about bowling but to my surprise they were not too enthusiastic about the bean bag toss.

Dr. T: Maybe the residents like bowling.

Dr. T: Do you still smoke?

Me: Yes, but I quit for 27 days and went back to smoking because the anxiety would build up and until it felt I would explode.

Dr. T: Did Champix work for you?

Me: It worked well but I was not willing to commit to the program because I know I would end with the anxiety again.

Dr. T: Sometimes it takes 2 years for Champix to work and you would have to pay for it.

Dr. T: Eighty percent of people living with Schizophrenia smoke and we do not know why. I do not know why?

Me: I can tell you why?

Dr. T: (Showing) Surprise and interest.

Me: Because it makes us feel normal.

Me: I have support when I am smoking.

Me: I shower everyday now and it takes me only 10 minutes not 25 minutes like before. I am not ritualistic in my bathing going over my body with the shower hose repeatedly anymore.

Dr. T: Go see your family doctor and he will help you out.

Dr. T: I will see you in three months.

Me: Goodbye.

Dr. T: Goodbye.

After I booked my next appointment with the secretary to see Dr. T. in three months I ran into the social worker who gave me individual therapy in the hallway at the hospital almost a year ago. We had a good chat and here is how it went.

Me: How are you Mike?

Mike: Good and you?

Me: Good.

Me: I heard you had a sickness.

Mike: I went through six weeks of chemotherapy treatments in Toronto.

Me: Good Toronto.

Mike: Yes, at the Princess Margaret Hospital.

Me: Is it gone.

Mike: No, they shrank it and I go for surgery next week.

Me: Good.

Me: Being friends with Gavin did not work out but I am friends with Dillon now.

Mike: I know. That is good.

Me: I need not write off my neighbors completely I just have to be around people who lift me up and do not bring me down.

Mike: Isn't that what everybody wants.

Me: I feel good now because I am on 7mg of Risperdal and got rid of Latuda cold turkey because it was not doing anything for me.

Mike: Your doctor recommended the adjustment.

Me: No, I just did it on my own.

Me: I knew Latuda was not working for me because I had to keep increasing my Risperdal I was taking with Latuda.

Mike: Well you know what you are doing.

Me: It was not a gamble because I have been on Risperdal in the past and it worked for me.

Me: The last few visits with my psychiatrist I was pressuring myself to remember what was being said at my appointments, then I had to keep telling myself I would remember everything when I got home to write it down, which I did. Our individual therapy appointment we had almost a year ago where we talked about the two wolves is in my new book.

Mike: We must get two copies for the waiting room.

Me: My book should be out around Christmas time.

Me: (Action) Shaking Mike's hand.

Mike: Take care.

Me: You too.

That night at 9:00pm, my friend Daniel called me, which is a rare thing for him to do. He lives a two hour's drive from me ever since he moved away from Peterborough a few years ago. He told me he sent me a book for my birthday and invited me up to his parents sailing boat for the weekend in August for his birthday. I told him I would not be attending, but told him to have a good time. He told me he has construction jobs in Peterborough he has to inspect and would be in town next Thursday and asked me if I wanted to go late lunch or early supper with him and I accepted.

# Chapter 6: Night Out

On Saturday July 29/2017, I hung out with my neighbors from my building outside in a grassy area at the side of the complex for an hour and had a good talk with them, then Dillon called inviting me to dinner for his brother Ricki's 59th birthday. Thirty minutes later, my neighbors complained about the other residents they did not get along with in the building and I took it as a sign to leave. I drove to Dillon's mothers Josie's place and arrived there in five minutes. Dillon was already there, as he took his mobility scooter and his brother Ricki and his girlfriend were there, as they came back from the east coast of Canada for a vacation via Pearson International Airport in Toronto in the afternoon. They brought with them fresh lobster and scallops for dinner. Dinner was good, but I do not know how to eat lobster and had to be shown how to crack the shell and retrieve the meat from the lobster. After dinner Dillon played six songs on his guitar and sang for everybody on the patio deck, but we had to go inside when it became dark outside, because the mosquitos were biting us. The only songs I recognized were: You Cannot Hide your Lien Eyes and Peaceful Easy Feeling by the Eagles. We had birthday carrot cake with cream cheese icing baked by Josie for dessert after the concert and everybody had a good time. Ricki and his girlfriend were tired from their travels so we called it an early night and I went home and Dillon went home simultaneously in his scooter.

My mother came up from Toronto on Monday, July 31$^{st}$/2017, by Greyhound bus and I picked her up at the bus terminal in the morning around 9:45am. She did a lot cleaning in my apartment, mostly dusting during the day, and then we went to McDonalds for dinner around 5:00pm. At the restaurant, the girl who took our order brought the food to us being guided by some GPS circle medallion placed on our table. My mom gave her a tip, as she thought she was in some fancy restaurant, it was funny. Then, my friend Dillon came over to my place for coffee, and my mom said that for the longest time she could not accept that I have Schizophrenia or I was thinking could not accept me because I have Schizophrenia. Dillon had a good talk with my mother and my mom peppered Dillon with questions and Dillon smoothly gave her, honest, caring and authentic answers in a humble way. My mom said to Dillon, David could have been anything, and Dillon said he still can and he is an author. Dillon stayed only 45 minutes, and after, my mom told me he was cool and a good friend, but was a little disappointed when he did not say she looked younger, by complimenting her, when she revealed her true age to him. My mom slept on my couch and said she had the best sleep ever because it is so quiet and peaceful unlike her apartment in uptown Toronto.

The next day my mother and I went to Talize: a used thrift store, where we bought nothing, but my mom tried on a pair of pants, but they did not fit her properly. Then, we went to Metro: a grocery store, to pick up a rump roast, some vegetables and two slices of watermelon. After eating the most delicious roast beef I ever had, we then went for a twenty-minute scenic drive beside the Otonabee river heading north towards an upscale tourist town called Lakefield and looped south towards Peterborough and stopped at a Giant Tiger a discount store on the highway before you enter the city limits. My mom did not like the clothes at the store and bought nothing there but I bought two polo shirts, some wine gums candy and a few scratch and win lottery tickets. My mom had another good sleep and in the morning around 10:00am I drove her to the bus terminal and thanked her for coming up and she said she must come up more often.

Friday August 4/2017, Dillon called me in the morning around 9:30 am, and asked me if I would drive him to pick up some Coffee-mate, and I told him I have to go to Walmart to pick up my prescriptions and we will go there. We ate at McDonalds, and again they brought the food to the table and Dillon wanted to give the hostess a tip, but she said she could not accept tips. After eating, Dillon asked me if I could drive him to the dollar store to pick up a birthday card for his middle brother Reggie, because he is coming to his mother's place for a visit on Sunday. After getting his card, Dillon asked me if there is anything else I want to do, and I told him I wanted to go to the liquor store and pick up some beer. My mother had given me a $25 liquor store gift card, and I wanted to use it up, because it was the long weekend, as it was the civic holiday. I went to the liquor store and bought two 6 packs of Old Milwaukee Ice Tall boy cans.

I was not planning on drinking the beer that day, but Dillon invited me out to a night on the town in the late afternoon. I went to my place and picked up the cold beer I had put in the fridge a few hours ago and we listened to John Prine at his place and drank two beers. Then Dillon sang on his karaoke machine Suspicious Minds by Elvis, but was having difficulty with the timing of the song, and trying to sing Elvis was hard for him even though he is a good singer, and I sang Crazy by Patsy Cline, where Dillon kept affirming me that is good when I would harmonize my voice.

About two hours at Dillon's place, we went out to the front of the building and called a cab. While the taxi was coming, Dillon told me to say a prayer: we will have a good time meet new people and that people will be attracted to and like us. While we were waiting, Dillon asked me if I knew who starred in the old Canadian show called The King of Kensington, and I told him I cannot remember who that was. The taxi arrived within ten minutes and Dillon asked the driver if he knew the name of the actor was, and the cab driver knew right away that it was Al Waxman.

We took about five minutes to get to our destination, Hunter street in Peterborough, the entertainment district of town, where we went first to a little bar. The Garnet had four people in it Dillon, me, a guy and the bartender. We talked about how the world is getting so automated and computer dependent there will be no jobs for anybody, because robots will be doing everything, including driving your car for you, which is already happening. We left there after forty minutes because I was hungry and wanted to get some food in me and this bar had a very limited food selection. At the Garnet, I had some peanuts and two bags of potato chips and a beer, so we moved on to an upscale bar and restaurant called 180 degrees with a patio facing Hunter street.

The waitress was cute serving us and was pleasant as we sat down right away in the only table but it was noisy there with people talking out loud and the Toronto Blue Jays baseball game was on the television trying to rally a comeback in the $6^{th}$ inning from 12 to 4 deficit to the Houston Astros.

We had two Caesars and I ordered the poutine. The fries were good and had lots of cheese curds, but they were not melted by the gravy as they should have been. Dillon was quiet there and I felt comfortable in my own skin and confident with no anxiety, fears or worries just having a quiet mind enjoying my time with my friend on the town. After I finished my meal, Dillon paid the bill, and then we moved on to a karaoke bar around the corner. Dillon told me after all the things I have done for him, he wanted to pay me back by treating me out to a night on the town, and I thought that was cool.

Within two minutes, we arrived at Tonic: the karaoke bar. Only about nine people in the place included the owner, bartender and karaoke technician and us. The karaoke machine was all tied up by an individual who had a few too many and mumbled the words to a few Elvis songs, until a group of about seven millennials came into the establishment. Dillon knew one guy because he knows Dillon's sister and Dillon told him to order anything he wants because it is his treat tonight. I ordered a Budweiser beer and Dillon ordered a Long Island Iced Tea with five white liquors. I asked for the book of songs to sing to be given, so I could sing a song, but I was so overwhelmed by the large selection, it left me confused. I saw one song The Sweetest Taboo by Sade and was contemplating singing that song, because I used to sing to her CD's when I was going to college in my younger years. The millennials singed to Katy Perry and Drake's song: Call me on my Cell phone and it was amusing seeing young people having a good time and it brought back how I used to be when I was younger. Then, Dillon went up and sang a Tim McGraw song: If You Are Reading This and he was good and after his performance the millennials were congratulating him and applauding him.

We went out for a cigarette and Dillon told me that the waitress at 180 degrees liked me, and I said cool. I told him I feel good and have good eye contact with women because I feel confident. He said girls like big guys, it makes them feel safe, and I said I was always intimidated by other people, but now I am not. He said I was giving him energy and motivation because I am his friend. I was feeling comfortable in my own skin at the karaoke place and not paranoid. I felt I belonged there and people liked me and I was not self-conscious. I was just another normal person, it was great. Dillon knows the owner of the bar and she was glad to see him, then Dillon asked me what time it was and I told him it was 1:00 am, and he said we better go to another bar. We ended up at The Only, and this bar has a large selection of craft beer and a large patio.

It was a Friday night, but the district was not too busy, because the University students are not in town yet and a rainstorm just finished when we arrived downtown. We walked in the bar and the stools were full of people, but we a found a space at the counter and Dillon picked up two beers. Then, we went outside to the patio and sat in a larger seating area, that could sit ten people, and it was just the two of us. A guy came out on his own, that was at the karaoke bar and said to Dillon: I like your singing and Dillon invited him to sit with us, but he declined, so Dillon offered to buy him a beer and gave him five dollars. That guy went into the bar and came out five minutes later with his friends. Dillon knew another guy Stewart, part of the friend's circle that included the guy Dillon bought a beer for, another guy and three girls. None of them were matched together and that they were all friends. Dillon invited them to sit with us and they were tentative but could not refuse the spacious seating before them.

They sat down and one guy talked about getting a place of his own because his landlord now does not allow him to have people over, even for a beer. We were talking about astrology signs and one girl said: she was a Pisces, and I said right on and told her we are old souls. Dillon then said: he was an Aries and another guy said: he was too. I said I got something off of Facebook that describes the signs in one sentence: and it says never stop an Aries. Dillon told the group, what I told him months ago, that Aries is the beginning and are always starting something and Pisces is the end and always finishing stuff off. Then a blonde girl in her middle 20's said out loud Hi Dillon and was excited to see him and gave him a big hug and that made Dillon look popular in front of the other people we were sitting with.

Two sisters were sitting beside me, and the one closest said: she likes Leonard Cohen and I asked her if she knew his song Hallelujah that KD Lang sang also. She sang a few words and I said cool.

Then I told her: I would sing Sade the Sweetest taboo at the karaoke bar, but felt I should not do it, because it is so romantic. She said: nothing is wrong with that and it would be like if she sang Frank Sinatra. I was really enjoying myself with the 30 year olds and felt comfortable and confident. I looked everybody in the eye when they looked at me and it seemed people liked me. Then, Dillon told the girl that was not one sister that I wrote three books, even though I have only two published and one is in the works, which is this book here, and have a psychology degree and she was impressed. I told her that my books are available on Amazon and she asked what are they about and I told her about mental health.

I overheard a few moments earlier the guy sitting across the table from me about how he works at telephone customer support company in town. So, later on I asked him: you work at Nordia and he did not want to talk with me and that was fine. I continued saying I worked at another telephone customer support company in town and the girl who was not the sister said that she works there now. I said I only lasted two months, because it was too stressful and she told me she just finished training and is just taking calls on the floor. I told her I took a call from a customer in the Yukon, who had recently lost her dad, and she said he was her best friend, and she had all photos of him were on her IPhone, but her screen was broken. I told her if she got to a computer, she could restore her photos from her IPhone. She cried while talking for thirty minutes and when I came home I wept for some time, because it was such an emotional phone conversation. The girl working at where I used to work said: she had a pot luck after training and brought in some beverages and I told her I brought a crockpot of my homemade chili and she was impressed again. I said at our pot luck I was the only person who brought real food everybody else just brought snacks. Dillon asked me: if I wanted another beer so he slipped me five dollars and I went up inside to the bar to get another beer. When I came back the two sisters went out to the front of the bar outside to have a cigarette and then Dillon went out with them too. When Dillon came back he said we should leave and he called a cab.

Outside in the front of the bar I was having a cigarette and I threw the butt in the gutter on the street like everyone else and a young woman in her middle 20's shouted at me: why did I do that and that I am a litterer. I told her I do not know why and kept quiet as she was ranting and raving. Dillon came to my defense and said that people get paid to clean the cigarette butts off the street and we keep them employed. She called him ignorant and Dillon said: I love you and she got even more mad. She quieted down when she knew she could not get a reaction out of us and left in a cab with her friends five minutes later. One sister when the girl left in the cab said: what was that all about and I told her I threw my cigarette butt in the street and she did not like it. Our cab we called must have been taken by that girl, so I just flagged a cab down and we went home.

It was around 2:00 am, and I told Dillon I will go to my place and pick up the other six tall boys beers in my fridge and grab a pack of smokes and continue the party. I had a few beers at Dillon's place and Dillon told me: there are a lot of lonely people and everybody does not have it all together. He also explained that people cannot stand it if you are clever and hate you if you are a fool and that we live in parallel universes. Dillon continued saying: where do you go when you have been insane. I said to Dillon: you are not a loser and he replied: thanking me and saying no one has ever spoken that. I left at around 5:00 am, and walked across the parking lot to my building, and took my bed time pills, and went to sleep.

# Chapter 7: Birthday Party

On Sunday August 8/2017, I went to Dillon's mothers Josie's place for Dillon's middle brother Reggie's 58th birthday with Dillon. We arrived there at 12:15 pm, where I was introduced to Reggie, his wife Debbie and their 16 years old daughter and Debbie's mother. Dillon's mother asked me: what was in my bag and I told her: it was books and she asked: what kind of books and I told her: it was my books the ones I have written. I told her: I would give Reggie both of my books signed for his birthday gift. Dillon gave his brother a birthday card and $50 liquor store gift card and Dillon's brother said: Dillon you should not have spent money on me, but appreciated the gift. Debbie asked: what is your book about and I replied: it is about Schizophrenia and she inquired: do you have Schizophrenia and I told her: yes. Debbie asked: where can people buy your book and I told her: it was on Amazon. Debbie asked: can you see and track your sales and I said: yes. Debbie asked: it must have been cathartic to write about your story and I told her: before I published my first book I was carrying around the story in my head and felt a release from the story when it got out into the world.

As our conversation ended I went into the kitchen away from the living room where Reggie was preparing lunch. I told him: I was on newer antipsychotics Abilify, Zeldox and Latuda at different times for four years and they did not work out. I then got stabilized on 7mg of Risperdal and he said how did your doctor know you needed the change and what to prescribe and I told him: I did it on my own and my doctor did not know about the change until a few months later. I knew Risperdal worked for me the past, so I just went back to my original medication. He said: doctors only know what you tell them they cannot know what is going on inside of you. I said: that I had to keep adding Risperdal to my newer medications and figured what are the newer medications doing if I have to keep increasing Risperdal.

I told Reggie: I knew Dillon for years because he lives in my neighborhood, but I did not know what to make of him, so I kept my distance as I did with most people in my area, and kept to myself when my newer medications were not working out. In the springtime I went into the gazebo near my building and met Dillon there and he invited me up for coffee and we exchanged telephone numbers and have been friends ever since. Dillon needs a good friend and you are better than his other friends. I said to Reggie: you give Dillon CD's and DVD's that includes a lot of country classic music. Often Dillon plays the music when I am at his place and I try to like and understand it, but it may take me awhile to get accustom to that music, and it must grow on me especially Merle Haggard when he talks about his wife leaving him or some sad song message he sings about.

After our conversation was over I went into the living room as Reggie stayed in the kitchen and Debbie's mother made a statement: that American authors write different than Canadians. I told her: my books do well in America and the U.K but not so much in Canada and I pointed out there is a greater population in those countries and regions than Canada and she agreed. Somehow we got on the topic about Joyce Meyer the Christian pastor and I told Debbie's mother: she has written many books about life and Christianity and came from an abused childhood and had a rough life to be a leader who has class, but is a real person. She said: she would look her up and I told her: she is on the Television about four times a day.

Reggie is a chef so he brought over some meals from his home in Oakville just west of Toronto for the birthday party. We had chicken sandwiches and salad with cherry tomatoes for lunch and then for dinner his homemade chili which included spices such as sage, sugar, cumin, garlic, chili powder and some other chili powder, cocoa powder and ingredients such as a can of beans, kidney beans, celery, sausage, ground pork and tomatoes and it was served with shredded marble cheese melted on the top of the chili. I had two bowls with sliced French bread with butter and it was good. For dessert we had Josie's carrot cake with cream cheese icing for lunch and it was scrumptious and for his birthday cake it was homemade rum cake that Debbie baked to perfection and made with lots of love because it was so moist.

Dillon and I shared two beers and the rest of the adults had white wine, but Reggie consumed no alcohol, because he was driving back home later that evening. Reggie was telling me: that some music or movies he copies for Dillon works on his PlayStation, Xbox and his computer but his DVD's sometimes do not work on Dillon's Sony DVD player. Recently he was using 8 Giga Byte dual layer DVD's and Dillon laser is probably too weak to read through the second layer on the DVD and thinks that is the issue.

I told Reggie: I tried to install my old Microsoft Word 2007 onto my Windows 10 computer and it would not allow it. I told him how Microsoft Word 2013 was hard to use because the page would jump to high when you scrolled up and too low when you scrolled down. I told him: I ruined two new computers when I installed Norton 360 antivirus while McAfee security was already installed on my Windows 10 laptop computer and they both crashed. He told me: next time disable or uninstall McAfee first before installing Norton.

I told Reggie: after I got my second laptop replaced through the in store warranty, my computer would stay stuck on restart mode and would not boot to the Windows desktop. I said I had to press the power button off and on to get the computer to boot. After time, that trick did not work anymore, so on my Samsung S5 neo I googled how to fix a computer stuck in restart mode. It told me: to hold the power button for three seconds three times with three seconds between to start the computer in safe mode. When I did that, it gave me an option to fix the computer, and I chose that selection, and the computer told me: it could not fix the problem, so I put the computer in safe mode again and I chose the selection to reinstall windows with the option to save my data. It worked, and my data was restored, but my favorites in my web browser Microsoft edge was gone.

Reggie said: he likes shooting games like Call of duty and does not like strategy games like SimCity and I told him: I like strategy games. I told him: I had SimCity 4 and it would not load on my Windows 10 laptop and it gave me an option after I installed it to choose compatibility mode, but I clicked the x at the top of the message window and closed it and never could get that window to pop up again. He told me to right click on the games desktop icon and choose properties, and it would give me an option to choose compatibility mode, but he further added that Windows 10 probably fixed that issue with recent updates and try to install it again.

Reggie told me: he closed his Facebook account for two years it got hacked into by someone in Thailand, so he contacted Facebook and expressed his concerns to them: how could his account get hacked into if it has been closed for two years, as he stated that obviously his information was still there. I told him: my computer got hacked into many years ago, as I had only one password for everything, and they got access to my email sending virus spam to my contacts list. I got a security breach warning form Facebook showing me a map of where the intruder was from in the world and it was South China. It told me: to change my password and I did.

I told Reggie: I erased old rough books I was thinking of writing and found them on Outlook 2011, when I searched for the title in the search space on my old Windows Vista desktop. He told me: that Windows computers' registries accumulate data and need to be cleaned, that is why Windows computers get slow after time, but he told me Apple computers have no registry. I said: is that like a temporary files folder and he said: no the registry was different. Reggie told me: that USB sticks are only supposed to last so long and to get new ones to back your pictures and data. I told him: when I am writing a book I always back it up on a USB stick.

I told Reggie: I texted Dillon and he called me by voice after and I was saying he was old fashioned and that I am too and understand. I told Dillon: it was easy to activate online banking on his IPhone and you can see all your transactions there. Dillon said: he uses phone banking and that is good enough for him and his brother agreed. Then, Reggie talked about: how he was shocked that Dillon texted him a message on his landline and a robot voice spoke the text message over his phone. I told Reggie: I had a friend Gilbert who would invite me to his regular Friday night poker games and would text my landline and a robot voice would speak saying please attend Poker at 7:00pm. I felt rejected by getting a robot message because I thought I was not important enough for my friend to talk with his own voice.

After my prolonged conversation with Reggie, Dillon jumped into the conversation and talked about: his cell phone and how he records music from his stereo to his IPhone and he has recorded himself singing and playing the guitar on his cellphone. Reggie was impressed and then Dillon played two his recorded songs for his brother and he liked them. Dillon then said: he went to the Bob Dylan concert in Oshawa just outside of Toronto and recorded almost the whole thing on his IPhone and it was a good recording. He said: Bob never spoke to the audience and just sang. Reggie said: that is good and that Bob Dylan need not say anything as he speaks through his music. I said to Reggie: when Dillon first got his IPhone 6s he forgot his passcode to get into his IPhone and I spent five hours setting up a Gmail account and an Apple id, then I installed ITunes on my computer and reset his IPhone. I told Reggie: I discovered how to do it by googling forgot passcode on an IPhone on my smartphone. We then went to Josie's computer and looked up Dillon either acting in a music video or playing music on YouTube.

The women were playing three games of scrabble, while us guys were talking about technology and looking up Dillon on the internet and according to the praises I heard that Josie won. Dillon and I went out for a smoke on the patio and it was hot out. I never felt the same coming in watching the Blue Jays game against the Houston Astros in Houston where the Blue Jays had 6-3 lead but lost 7-6 in the 9$^{th}$ inning. I took 1mg of Risperdal because I was not feeling so good and felt closed off to people and just stared at the Television. I was just out of center because we had been there almost six hours and the socializing was a little too much to handle for such a long time. Debbie asked: Dillon and myself what do we do with our time and he told her: we go out for a bite to eat or grocery shop and that we went out for a night on the town Friday. Dillon said everywhere he goes young women are screaming his name and hugging him. Debbie said: you must like that that Dillon and Dillon downplayed it by saying: I do not know why they love me so much and I do not even know who they are. I was not feeling that great and Dillon was tired so we left at 6:30pm where I said goodbye to everybody either shaking hands or hugging and receiving kisses. Dillon's mother gave me four yellow muffins topped with chocolate crème cheese icing to take home with me. I drove home and Dillon and I parted ways.

# Conclusion

I was mildly psychotic for four years because my medication switches to newer anti-psychotic medications did not work out. I became over sensitive to other people's offenses and wore an emotional protective shell to shelter me from others. I harbored un-forgiveness, thinking I was hurting those who have wounded me emotionally, but I was only injuring myself. I was prideful and was judgmental and pushed people out of my life because of it. I was alone for those years because I had such a self-righteous and poor attitude. I expected God to bless me financially so I could run away from everybody, the town and everything I knew. I was unwell and put a lot of pressure on myself because my real-self did not match my ideal-self. That gap in my Self and being alone polluted my perspective towards myself, others and life. I felt rejected, hurt and abandoned and did not know what to do to fix my unfair situation and restore my health.

It was not until I reached out for help that my perspective changed for the better. I got desperate enough I confided in my psychiatrist about my problems and sought emotional support from group and individual therapy. My psychiatrist guided me in the right direction by revealing that I needed more social support, but the decision to change my medication was mine. Group therapy was too superficial and politically correct to help me out, but getting things off my chest was a big relief, even though I may have offended other people in the group. Individual therapy was an intelligent session and it made me feel good to communicate with someone on a deeper intellectual level talking about the ego than my regular everyday conversations with my family. This was a turning point towards my recovery, but it was not until I forgave others and changed my medication to 7mg of Risperdal I became stable in my mental health and my life improved.

Then, I became friends with Dillon and felt accepted and my life took off for the better. My love tanks were restored and I found it easier to be friendly towards others and not be so self-conscious. Dillon and myself have a lot in common and I have met many people doing things with Dillon. Dillon and I understand each other, that we both need positive emotional support that can only come from someone who knows what it is like to live with a mental illness. Our mental health is improving day by day and knowing I am wanted, needed and belong is a great contributor to how I am feeling today. My family do not annoy and offend me anymore because I am healthy and stable. I see the good in them and accept them for who they are. That makes it easier for them to emotionally support me and that makes us all happy. It shows that my family cares because they feel confident in my abilities because I got out the rut I was in. I took chances and had leap of faith trusting God by being social again, being friends with Dillon and having the courage to volunteer at the retirement home.

I am easy on myself now and in return I am easy on other people. I have found that attitude is everything these days and having a judgmental attitude just returns to you twice the strength and what you are trying to escape just gets larger. If you have your head in the sky or nose in the air people will avoid you or try to bring you down off your pedestal. I am not prideful anymore because I am not trying to compensate for being alone and sick wanting to be a different person and having a different life. When you have a lot of pride I think it is because you think you are more than what you are. I do not magnify out of proportion the flaws of myself and others because I have more than a few and other people do to. I try to look at the good things about people and it is a lot easier to do when you have the right attitude. I took a long time to accept myself having Schizophrenia especially since when I was not feeling too good my awareness of stigma increases.

I do not feel vulnerable and forsaken anymore because I have a friend in Dillon and am social again. People accept me because I accept myself and in return can accept others for who they are imperfections and all. Self-acceptance is the key to wellness for anybody especially someone living with a disability. Everybody needs to feel needed and wanted and I have that now and that has made all the difference in my life. People can have millions of dollars and be miserable and unhappy because they have not found acceptance. The key to life's secret to happiness is to match your real-self with your ideal-self knowing that God knows who you are, where you are and where you are going. Setting and achieving goals gives you power and purpose for your life and erases negative emotions such as helplessness, and I do that by enjoying my walk with the Lord and writing about my experiences.

Made in the USA
Monee, IL
23 August 2020